Of

Bl

Bob Hartman knows how to captivate an audience, and regularly entertains children and adults around the world as a performance storyteller. He is perhaps best known for the widely acclaimed *Lion Storyteller Bible*. When he is not writing, Bob enjoys making music, reading about classic cars, and entertaining his grandchildren.

Published by Lion Children's Books
an imprint of
Lion Hudson plc
Wilkinson House, Jordan Hill Road,
Oxford OX2 8DR, England
www.lionhudson.com/lionchildrens

ISBN 978 0 7459 6556 7
e-ISBN 978 0 7459 6822 3

First edition 2015

A catalogue record for this book is available from the British Library

Printed and bound in the UK, February 2015, LH26

Off-the-Wall
BIBLE TALES

Retold by Bob Hartman
Illustrated by Woody Fox

LION
CHILDREN'S

CONTENTS

INTRODUCTION

When I teach people how to tell stories, one of the things I always mention is "playfulness". Playfulness in the act of telling and also in the creation of the retelling.

I think that's particularly important with Bible stories, because the assumption of the audience is that a Bible story will likely be serious, moral-laden, preachy, and dull.

So when I retell Bible stories, I look for elements in the stories that counter those stereotypes. And, guess what, they are not hard to find. There is wonder. And there is adventure. And there is lots and lots of humour.

Focusing on those elements does not diminish the importance or the message of the story. On the contrary; by getting the reader or listener to laugh and wonder, it opens them up to the truth within.

The stories in this book are all examples of my attempt to play with the Bible. The "play" takes different forms, depending on the story. Sometimes it's in the repetition. Sometimes it's in the characters. Sometimes (as in the case of the Creation story) it comes from asking a simple question of the story. "If God spoke the world into existence, what words might he have used?"

I think that you and your children will get the most out of these stories if you receive them with that intent in mind – if you see the Bible as a book to be enjoyed, and asked questions of, and mined for humour. A book to be played with. Seriously.

Bob Hartman

IT ALL STARTS HERE

Genesis 1-2

At first everything was dark. And everything was quiet.

SHHHH.

Not a whisper. Not a peep. Not a sound.

So God cried, "Light!"

Everything went bright.

And he separated the day from the night.

God gurgled, "Sea."

Gently sighed, "A Pale Blue Sky."

Then chuckled, "Heavens!" in wonder – and
there they were.

God bellowed next, "Earth!" – deep and loud
and strong.

And out of the deep the mountains rose and
the dry land followed along.

"Bloom!" God boomed. And plants and trees
and bushes shot up from the
ground. Then, from their
stalks and stems and
branches, sprang
flowers and fruit.

He shouted, "Shining
Sun!"

He howled, "Harvest
Moooooon."

And when he sang,
"Stars," they tinkled
and twinkled in tune.

God glugged and chattered and splashed, and a seaful of fish burst through the waves, flipping and flapping in return.

Then God chirped and quacked and shrieked, and a skyful of birds appeared in answer, echoing back his call.

And when he roared and baaed and mooed and mewed, the animals sprang forth and joined his roaring chorus.

"Just one more thing to do," God thought.

And he looked at the dust and whispered, "Hello, Man!"

He looked again and whispered, "Hello, Woman!" as friendly as you like.

And when they stood up to greet him, God said, "This world is for you. It's noisy, but it's good. Fill it with children. And take care of it for me."

And then, his work done, God rested and smiled and said, "Aaaaah!"

LAUGHTER

Genesis 12, 15, 17–18, 21

"Abraham!" God called. "Oh, Abraham!"

And Abraham did what you do when God calls your name.

He said, "Yes, Lord?"

"Abraham," God said. "Oh, Abraham. I want to make you the father of a very special family. I want to give you more children than there are stars in the sky. I want to give you more children than there are grains of sand on the seashore. And your children, Abraham, your children will bless the whole world!"

Abraham was more than a little surprised by this. He was seventy-five years old, you see. And his wife, Sarah, was nearly as old as him – far too old to have children. But Abraham trusted God, that's the thing. So he asked God, "What do you want me to do?"

"Abraham, oh Abraham," God said. "Pack up your things. Your tents and your animals and all you have. And follow me. I have a special place I want to take you, and a special land I want to give you. That's my promise."

So Abraham did what you do when God asks you to pack up your things. He packed up his things, saddled up his beasts, gathered his relatives, and left his home and followed God to the land of Canaan.

Twenty-five years went by. Abraham was a hundred now, and still he and Sarah had no children.

There was his tent. His old wife was working inside. There was the sun, beating down on him in the middle of the day. But all Abraham could think about was God's promise: *I want to give you more children than there are stars in the sky or grains of sand on the seashore.* It seemed more impossible than ever. So Abraham wondered – when would the promise come true?

And then something happened. Three men came walking by, and all Abraham knew was they had something of God about them. They might have been very holy men. They might have been angels. They might somehow have been God himself.

Abraham bowed before them and then offered to wash their feet and bring them something to eat.

And when they accepted, he knew.

"Abraham, oh Abraham," they said. "That's very kind of you."

Abraham hurried into the tent and asked Sarah
to bake some bread. Then he hurried to his
herd of cows and picked a calf and asked a
servant to kill it and to cook it. Then he hurried
back to his guests and served them the meal.
For a man of a hundred, hurrying was hard!

As they ate, the visitors asked him a question.
    "Abraham, oh Abraham, where is Sarah,
your wife?"
    "There, in the tent," Abraham answered.
    And then it happened. The thing that
Abraham had been waiting for.

"We will come back next year," said the guests. "And by the time we do, Sarah will have a son."

Now Sarah wasn't at the back. No, she was right up front, sitting at the entrance. Listening in on the conversation between Abraham and his special guests!

And when she heard what the guests had to say, she couldn't believe it. "I'm too old," she thought. "Far too old to have a child." And then she giggled. And then she chuckled. And then she laughed right out loud. So loudly, in fact, that the guests heard her!

"Sarah is laughing!" they said. "Does she not know that there is nothing too hard for God? Trust us; when we come back next year, she will indeed have a child."

And a year later, she did!

Sarah. Old Sarah. Nearly-a-hundred-years-old Sarah. Sarah, well beyond childbearing age, gave birth to a baby boy. And when she did, she laughed again − for joy this time. So she called the boy "laughter", which is what his name, Isaac, means.

A BOBBING BABY

Exodus 1-2

There was a baby bobbing in a bulrush basket, hiding in the riverside reeds.

Why?

Because he was a Hebrew.

Because he was a boy.

Because he was born in Egypt.

And because Pharaoh, the ruler of Egypt, had decided that there were too many Hebrews, so every baby Hebrew boy should be killed.

There was a baby bobbing in a bulrush basket, hiding in the riverside reeds.

Why?

Because his mum was clever.

Because she loved him very much.

Because he cried when she tried to hide him, so she had to find a better way to save his life.

There was a baby bobbing in a bulrush basket, hiding in the riverside reeds.

Why?

Because his mum made a baby-sized basket out of bulrushes.

Because she coated it with tar to keep the water out.

Because she placed it in the reeds, near the water's edge, so no one would see, and asked his big sister to watch over him.

There was a baby bobbing in a bulrush basket, hiding in the riverside reeds.

Pharaoh's daughter knew why. She knew all about the rule her father had made.

But when she went bathing by the river

and when she saw the basket
and when she heard the baby cry
and when she lifted him out of the basket and
saw that he was a Hebrew
she loved him anyway.

There was a baby bobbing in a bulrush basket,
hiding in the riverside reeds.

But now that he was no longer hiding, his
sister had to do something.

She popped up from her own hiding place
and she spoke to Pharaoh's daughter.

"If you want someone to nurse the baby," she
said, "I know a Hebrew woman who would be
happy to do it."

"Fetch her at once!" the princess replied.

There was a baby bobbing in a bulrush basket, hiding in the riverside reeds.

And now he was being handed to his own mum by the daughter of the man who wanted him dead!

"Nurse this baby for me," said Pharaoh's daughter. "And I'll pay you for your trouble." (As if the story couldn't get any better!)

So the baby's mum nursed him and cared for him and when he was old enough, she took him to the palace.

"He was just a baby bobbing in a bulrush basket, hiding in the riverside reeds," said Pharaoh's daughter. "And I pulled him out and I gave him a name – a name that means 'pulled out'."

And that's why she called him "Moses".

THE VOICE

1 Samuel 3

Samuel was just a boy, but he had a very important job. He worked in Shiloh, at the tabernacle, where people came to worship God. He worked for the old priest Eli and slept in the tabernacle.

One night, as the lamplight in the tabernacle burned bright, Samuel was awakened by a voice – a voice that called his name.

So Samuel got out of bed. And he ran to the side of old Eli.

"You called me. I'm here," said Samuel.

Eli rubbed his eyes. He was nearly blind. And when he saw it was Samuel, he said, "I didn't call you. Go back to bed."

Samuel was confused. He left old Eli. And he lay back down on his bed.

But just as he closed his eyes, the voice called his name again.

Samuel jumped out of bed. And he woke old Eli again.

"I'm here," he said. " You called me."

"I did no such thing, my boy," old Eli replied. "Back to bed."

So, nervously, Samuel did as he was told. He left old Eli. And slipped back into bed.

The lamplight flickered. And the voice called once more.

Samuel leaped out of bed, this time. And he raced back to old Eli.

"You called me," the boy said, trembling. "I'm here!"

Eli's weak eyes moved back and forth, like he was searching for something. Then he shut those eyes and nodded.

"I know," he said. "I know exactly who is calling you. He hasn't spoken for a very long time, but I think God wants to speak to you tonight. So the next time you hear him call, say, 'What do you want, Lord? Your servant is ready to listen.' "

Samuel was amazed. And just a little scared.

But he trusted old Eli. So he left the old priest. And just as his head hit the pillow, God called his name.

"Samuel. Samuel."

"What do you want, Lord?" Samuel replied. "Your servant is ready to listen."

"I have so much to tell you," God said. "Words for my people. Words that will make their ears tingle and change them for ever. Will you listen to my words, Samuel? And will you pass them on?"

Samuel nodded, "Yes."

And the words never stopped coming, until Samuel was an old man himself.

BIG AND LITTLE

1 Samuel 17

David was a boy. A little shepherd boy.

One day, he took a big pile of bread and a big chunk of cheese to his big brothers, who were soldiers in the army.

While David's big brothers were munching on their big lunch, they looked up and saw a Big Giant. With a Big Giant Spear. And a Big Giant Shield. And a Big Giant Helmet.

"Send someone to fight me!" said the Big Giant with a Big Giant Roar.

Now David may only have been a little shepherd boy. But he trusted in a Great Big God.

So he stood up and with a little voice

announced, "I will fight the Big Giant."

It was a Big Shock to his Big Brothers, and all the other soldiers, too.

So they took the little shepherd boy to see their Big King, Saul.

Saul thought it was a Big Joke at first. But David wasn't laughing.

So King Saul offered to help him.

He put his Big Armour on the little shepherd boy.

He put his Big Helmet on, too.

But they were Big. Too Big!

"I don't need your Big Armour," said David to King Saul. "When a Big Lion and a Big Bear tried to eat my little sheep, Great Big God helped me beat them. And he  will help me beat this Big Giant, too!"

So David, the little
shepherd boy,
went to a little
stream. He
found one,
two, three,
four, five little
stones. He put
them in his little bag,
along with his little
sling. And he set
off to fight the Big
Giant.

David, the little
shepherd boy,
looked at the Big
Giant. He looked at his Big Spear. He looked at
his Big Shield. He looked at his Big Helmet.

Then the Big Giant looked at David. And
laughed a Big Laugh.

"You send a boy, a little shepherd boy, to fight
me?" the Big Giant roared.

"Is that a stick?

"Am I a dog?

"I will feed his little body to the birds!"

Then David, the little shepherd boy, prayed a little prayer.

"Help me, Great Big God."

And he put a little stone into his little sling.

Then he gave it a little spin, and then a little fling.

And the little stone flew through the air further…

and a little further…

and a little further still…

till it struck the Big Giant in the middle of his Big Forehead.

And he fell with a Big Thud to the ground.

David's Big Brothers gave a Big Cheer. And so did the rest of the soldiers.

But the little shepherd boy just bowed his head and prayed, "Thank you, Great Big God!"

BROTHERS

2 Kings 4

Daniel peeped out of the window. He was only eight, and just tall enough to stand on his tiptoes and stick his nose up over the sill.

His little brother, Micah, was just six, and he wanted to see as well. So he pulled a stool to his brother's side and climbed up on it, rocking back and forth as he went.

"Watch out!" Daniel complained.

"But I want to see Mum too!" moaned Micah. And he stuck his nose over the sill as well, with a "What's she doing?"

"She's talking to that man," explained Daniel. "She said his name is Elisha. He's a prophet – like dad was."

"My husband was a prophet, just like you," the boys' mum told Elisha, wiping her eyes with her sleeve. "But he's dead now. And, when he died, he owed a lot of money. They came to me, the people he owed money to – they want to take everything we have to pay off part of the debt. And they want to sell my boys as slaves to pay off the rest."

Elisha looked past her to the two lumps of curly black hair that kept bobbing up and down at the bottom of her window.

"So there's nothing left?" asked the prophet.

"A bit of oil," the woman shrugged. "That's all."

The prophet grinned. "That will do nicely."

"I told you to stop rocking!" Daniel shouted. "I told you you'd fall down!"

"I'm okay," grunted Micah, picking himself up off the floor and rubbing one elbow.

"But you broke the stool!" Daniel shouted again. "Mum is going to be really angry!"

Just at that moment, she came bursting back into the house.

"Boys!" she announced. "I've got something for you to do."

"Micah broke the stool!" shouted Daniel.

And Micah started to cry.

"It's all right," she said, giving him a hug. "Really. You have to borrow jars. Empty jars. As many as you can. From everyone in the village."

"But why?" asked Daniel.

"Because Elisha said so. Now, go!"

So they went – one brother up the street and the other down, banging on doors, borrowing jars, and juggling them in their arms all the way back home.

Micah dropped a couple on the way. And

Daniel sighed and shook his head.

But, several trips later, when they had begged and bothered and pestered every neighbour, their house was filled with jars.

The boys' mum took what little oil she had and poured it into one of the jars until the jar was full.

"I don't get it," said Daniel. "There wasn't enough oil to do that."

"I know," said his mum. "The prophet just told me to keep on pouring."

So she did. And before they knew it, the second jar was full! And the one after that!

"Let me try," said Micah.

And, one by one, they filled the jars on the floor and on the chairs and on the table. Every jar in the house!

"What do we do now?" asked Daniel, tiptoeing around the jars.

"We sell what we can and we keep what's left for ourselves," answered his mum. "I think that should be enough to take care of us for a long time."

"And to buy a new stool?" asked Micah sheepishly.

"Maybe even two," his mother grinned.

And she hugged them both and held them tight.

"One for each of my boys."

SURPRISE!

Matthew 1–2; Luke 1–2

Mary was at home, just minding her own
business, when…
SURPRISE!

An angel named Gabriel appeared.
"You're going to have a baby, Mary," the
angel said. "And he will be God's own Special
Son."

Mary was engaged to Joseph the carpenter.
He did not believe her story. So while he was
sleeping one night…

SURPRISE!

The angel appeared to him, too, in his dreams.

"Mary is telling the truth," the angel said. "The baby she is carrying is indeed God's Son. Call him Jesus when he is born. He will save his people from their sins."

So Joseph married Mary and her belly grew and grew until, one day…

SURPRISE!

They heard that everyone had to go back to their hometown to be counted by the government.

So off they went to Bethlehem, Joseph's hometown, and a long journey from where they lived.

When they arrived, it was almost time for the baby to be born. They looked for a place to stay when they got there, but the inns were all full.

And then…

SURPRISE!

A kindly innkeeper found them a place to sleep in his stable. And…

SURPRISE!

That's where God's own Special Son was born.

There were poor shepherds in the fields that night, minding their own business and minding their sheep, when...

SURPRISE!
The angel Gabriel appeared to them, too.
"Your Special Saviour has been born," the angel told them. "The one you have been waiting for. He's in a stable in Bethlehem, lying in a manger."

Then…
SURPRISE!
Gabriel was joined by an angel choir.
"Praise God!" they sang. "And peace to everyone on earth."

So off they went to Bethlehem, and just as the angel told them…
SURPRISE!
God's own Special Son wasn't sleeping in a palace or a mansion or even a proper house. He was lying in a manger, in a lowly place where animals kept warm through the night.

Far, far away, stargazers spotted something strange in the sky…
SURPRISE!

A shooting star!

"If we follow it," they said, "it will lead us to a king."

So off they went, across the desert, and the star led them, at last, to Bethlehem.

The baby was older now, and the family had found a little house.

It was still nothing special, but the stargazers knew different. They knew there was a king inside. So, when they entered, they gave the baby presents fit for a king: gold and frankincense and myrrh.

And the stargazers bowed.

And the baby smiled.

And Mary just sat and wondered at all that God had done.

SURPRISE!

WHAT WRECKED THE ROOF?

Matthew 9; Mark 2; Luke 5

There was a crowd in the house.

Elbows in ears. Knees in noses. So tight you could hardly move.

Jesus was making sick people well.

And, just like me, everyone wanted to see.

There was a crowd in the house.

There was a hole in the roof.

Plaster falling. Dust spreading. People sneezing. Faces peeping through.

Four men had a friend who couldn't walk. They tore the hole there so they could get their friend to Jesus.

There was a crowd in the house.

There was a hole in the roof.

There was a man on the floor who couldn't walk.

His friends had put him on a mat and lowered him through the hole. He looked up at Jesus.

And Jesus looked down at him and said, "Your sins are forgiven, friend."

There was a crowd in the house.

There was a hole in the roof.

There was a man on the floor who couldn't walk.

There was a gang of religious leaders who weren't very happy.

They muttered and mumbled and grumbled.

"Who does Jesus think he is?" they said. "Only God can forgive sins."

There was a crowd in the house.

There was a hole in the roof.

There was a man on the floor who couldn't walk.

There was a gang of religious leaders who weren't very happy.

There was a cheeky grin on Jesus' face.

He looked at the religious leaders and said, "God has given me permission to forgive this man – to fix what's wrong in his heart. And

to prove it, I'll fix what's wrong with his legs."

Then he said to the man on the mat, "Get up and walk."

There was a crowd in the house.

There was a hole in the roof.

There was a man on the floor who couldn't walk.

There was a gang of religious leaders who weren't very happy.

There was a cheeky grin on Jesus' face.

There was a lame man walking out the door.

Except he wasn't lame anymore. When Jesus

told him to get up, he did! Then he picked up
his mat, the crowd parted, and out of the house
he went.

There was a crowd in the house.

There was a hole in the roof.

There was a man on the floor who couldn't
walk.

There was a gang of religious leaders who
weren't very happy.

There was a cheeky grin on Jesus' face.

There was a lame
man walking out the
door.

There was a
cheering crowd.
And I cheered
loudest of all.

Because the lame
man walking was
my dad!

THOMAS'S TUMMY

John 6

Thomas's tummy was rumbling. It was always rumbling, to be fair, because Thomas was a growing boy. But it was rumbling particularly hard today, because he had just walked up the side of a mountain!

There were thousands of other people who had walked up the mountain as well. That's because Jesus was on the mountain, and the people knew that he was able to make sick people well again. They wanted to be there when it happened. And Thomas did, too.

Thomas's tummy rumbled again and he reached for one of the little loaves of bread his mother had baked for him.

He only had five to last him the whole day. And a couple of small dried fish. So he knew he had to make them stretch.

But just as he was about to take a bite, someone spoke to him.

"My name is Andrew," the man said. "I'm one of Jesus' disciples. I don't suppose you would mind sharing your food, would you?"

Thomas stared at the bread. He did mind, actually. His tummy was roaring now. But his parents had always told him that sharing was a good thing to do. So he handed his lunch to Andrew.

"Jesus!" Andrew called. "I have a boy here with, let's see… five barley loaves and two fish. I don't see how they'll stretch to feed everyone, though."

"Everyone?" wondered Thomas. "If Jesus wants to share my lunch with everyone, I won't get anything to eat at all." And his tummy gave a disappointed rumble in reply.

"Tell the crowd to sit down." Jesus said to his disciples. And when they had – thousands

and thousands of them – Jesus took the bread,
thanked God for it, then started breaking it into
pieces. He did the same with the fish. And as
Thomas watched, his mouth dropped open and
his eyes grew wide. For the more bread and the
more fish that Jesus broke, the more there was!

Enough to feed everyone, and more besides.

"Gather up the leftovers," Jesus told his disciples. "No point in letting good food go to waste."

And, somehow, they managed to fill up twelve baskets full.

When the work was finished, Andrew wiped his forehead and nudged Thomas.

"Aren't you going to eat that?" he asked.

And Thomas looked at the food in his lap.

Five little loaves. Two dried fish.

"I... umm... wow!" muttered Thomas. "That was amazing."

"Yeah," Andrew nodded. "Jesus has a way of surprising people like that.

"But you know what?" he added. "He needed what you did, too. So thanks for sharing."

And then Thomas's tummy rumbled again.
So he reached for his food and ate it all up.
It was, in so many ways, the best lunch ever!

A SHEEP STORY

Luke 15

We know that Jesus told lots of stories — stories that we call parables. But we don't actually know where Jesus got the ideas for his stories. This story is just a fun little guess about one of those stories.

The shepherd boy walked slowly up the hill, looking for his little lost sheep. The sun was setting — an orange ball teetering on the top of the hill. It would be dark soon. And cold. He needed to hurry.

He looked behind a bush. But all he found was a lizard.

He looked behind a boulder. But all he found were a pair of feeding birds.

Then he looked behind a tree on the hilltop. And there was a man!

"What are you looking for?" the man asked.

"My lost sheep," answered the boy.

And the man smiled. "Then I will help you."

They looked behind another bush. But all they found was a snake.

They looked behind another boulder. But all they found was a rock badger.

The sun was just a semicircle now, and the boy was getting nervous.

BAA!

Then they both heard a "baa" and raced to where the hill dropped off into a rocky ravine.

There was the sheep, on a ledge, tangled in a trap of thorn bushes. So the boy climbed down, and the man followed, gingerly picking his way.

Knife out, the boy cut away the branches, then hoisted the sheep onto his shoulders.

The man lent a hand, and they climbed back up to safe ground.

"Is that your only sheep?" the man asked.

The boy shook his head and pointed back down the hill. "No. We've got a hundred. Right down there."

"Then that one must be pretty special," the man replied, "for you to go to all that trouble when you have so many more."

The shepherd boy shifted the sheep on his shoulders and smiled.

"My dad says they're all special. Why do you think he sent me here?"

"I understand," the man smiled back. "I've got a dad like that, too."

Then the boy turned and headed back to the sheepfold.

And Jesus followed the setting sun down the other side of the hill to the town below.

WAITING

Matthew 19; Mark 10; Luke 18

Joshua tossed a rock into the air.

Jael jabbed a leaf with a stick.

Jacob jumped up, just as high as he could.

"Mum, why are we standing in this queue?" asked Jonah.

Joshua caught the rock with one hand.

Jael nearly squashed a passing ant.

Jacob tried to stand on his head.

"We're waiting to see Jesus," Mum told Jonah.

Joshua drew a stickman in the sand.

Jael chased after a toad.

Jacob landed with a thud on his bottom.

"But why is it taking so long?" asked Jonah.

Joshua saved the toad from Jael.

Jael crossed her arms and sulked.

Jacob cried and Mum picked him up.

"Jesus is very busy," she told Jonah. "He's making sick people well. But our turn will come. And when it does, he'll pray to God and ask him to watch over you."

Joshua held the toad in the air.

Jael whacked Joshua on the arm.

Jacob put a handful of sand in his mouth.

"You have to go away," said one of Jesus' helpers to Jonah and his mum. "Jesus is too busy to see you."

Joshua dropped the toad on the ground.

Jael tried to catch it.

Jacob spit out the mouthful of sand.

Then Jesus walked up to Jonah and his mum.

"Don't send these children away!" he told his helper. "I want them to come to me. God's kingdom is made up of people just like them."

Then Jesus prayed for Joshua and Jacob and Jonah and Jael. He asked God to watch over them.

And the toad hopped safely away.

EUTYCHUS YAWNED

Acts 20

Eutychus yawned.

It had been a long day.

He'd risen early and done his chores.

Then run himself ragged, playing with his friends.

But now it was late, really late.

Eutychus yawned and yawned.

It's not that he was bored.

It was Paul, after all, who was talking.

Paul, who had persecuted the followers of Jesus.

Paul, who had met Jesus himself, in a blinding vision on the road – and had come to follow him, too.

Paul, who had travelled the world, telling everyone about Jesus' life and death and resurrection and doing miracles in his name.

It was Paul who was talking. But he'd been talking for a long time – and it was nearly midnight.

Eutychus yawned and yawned and yawned.

The smoke from the lamps didn't help.

It burned his eyes and made him drowsy.

So he climbed onto the wide sill of an open window, perched three storeys above the street below, to get a little air.

And still Paul kept talking.

Eutychus yawned and yawned and yawned and yawned.

And then he stopped yawning.

And started sleeping.

And snoring. He slumped, and then slipped

off the sill and fell out of the window to the ground below.

People screamed.

Paul stopped talking.

And everyone raced down the three flights of stairs to the street.

"He's dead!" someone shouted.

But Paul scooped him up in his arms and said different.

"Don't be alarmed." he cried. "The boy's alive."

And so he was!

Some of the people went back upstairs and Paul carried on with his talk. He didn't finish until daybreak!

And the rest of the people?

They took Eutychus home.

And made sure he got to bed.

"You're lucky to be alive," they said. "It's a good thing Paul was there."

And Eutychus nodded.
And Eutychus smiled.
And Eutychus yawned.
And yawned.
And yawned.
And yawned.
And yawned.
Then fell safely back to sleep.